CONTENTS

Understanding	4
The Start	9
Entropy	12
Who Is the Master?	21
U-Turn	28
Factors Which Escalate and Worsen	32
Alignment	43
Staying Sober	50
To New Beginnings	54

About Author

The author is a holder of a science degree in agriculture. He got initiated into addiction at the age of thirteen and has since struggled with the disease. He changed high schools four times after getting into trouble because of the disease. He got caught up in a group of addicts in the city where he got introduced to heavier substances. He lost control after the substance abuse caught up to him and so he dropped out of school and went to a rehabilitation centre. After being clean, he enlightened himself and broadened his mind in the year and a half which he spent at home. He went back to school in his twenties, only to find that the school curriculum had changed and so instead of completing his matric as intended, he was obligated to go back to grade 10. He relapsed but due to the skills which he had taught himself while he was a dropout, combined with the skills he acquired from rehab, he was able to acquire 6 distinctions for his matric. He went to university where the disease engulfed him further but he was later able to subdue his addiction without specialist intervention.

Preface

Remember in high school when you had to read a book and got questioned during exams on it, and those questions made you realize that you didn't understand the book in the way that you thought you did? Well here I intend to tame that – this is a learning book which seeks for you to understand without a doubt what is being said. When young, your parent/guardian might tell you not to drink or use drugs and tell you about the local addict who has nothing but a rapidly fading lifespan. You then happen to see a group of highly successful people, drinking and smoking at the local pub or on the television thus you start doubting the truth in the words of your mother - what is the difference between these achievers and non-achievers?

I'm not here to tell you to stop nor to start using because that's none of my business but what I can say is that: if you are going to do it, you might as well do it right. The inspiration behind this book was looking back at the mistakes that I made as a teenager, and realizing that there was a number of youngsters who were in the same drug infested boat as I, some of them being in one rivalling an ark. I am one of them because I understand that it is a lifelong battle, but I have been able to subdue it and make strides of progress.

During the course of fighting and subduing, I had to learn as much as possible about my enemy because that is the only way you can beat such an experienced heavyweight who has a one punch knockout power. Addiction is broad because everyone is an addict in one way or the other, but I will focus more on substance addiction although not exclusively, and when I'm drunk on the subject, possibly reveal people's secrets because "a drunk mind speaks a sober heart".

The intention is to educate those who are coming, open the eyes of those that are before me and use a machete to make a path that leads to salvation for my fellows - not because I'm some hero but because a spirit within me would not let me progress in peace before writing this piece. With repetitions, because "repetition is the father of learning", we are going to unpack this dramatization in an individual, of an environment, with his perception of the environment, including agitators which enhance substance use and this will allow the reader to understand. This can also be done on other individuals from different environments.

UNDERSTANDING

If only certain things were only learnt and not past on genetically maybe then there wouldn't be a need for this book and my father would not have passed away at the age of 29 due to complications that came about through his addiction, as a result I wouldn't still be waiting for him to come back for me, as he had promised during the one and only time that I met him. Most people think that addicts are just morally flawed people who chose the life that they lead but what one must realize is that two people with a similar background and the same age could try out alcohol today and one of them would wake up the following day hooked, whilst the other would actually be disgusted or feel indifferent even. The objective truth is that drug addicts/alcoholics are no different from people who suffer from depression or other mental disorders and should not be treated differently because these are the same; in the same way that you can't just tell a person who is depressed to just stop, it is the same with addiction. The illness is hereditary, and genes have been identified which are the cause; I would go as far as saying that everyone has addiction genes, but they vary from person to person(polygenic).

Research from the National Institute of Health suggests that those who suffer from other mental disorders are more susceptible to addiction than those who don't. The environment has a big influence on the road to induction and management. To someone who did not inherit it: the more pain, trauma , stress or any long term imbalance in your internal environment that builds up in you, the more susceptible you are to an addiction because the substance serves as a counter to the unwanted imbalance by helping you release dopamine(the 'feel good' hormone).

Let's take a step back. If you are experiencing hard times, using a substance that releases dopamine into your mind would ease the pain and struggle – thus balancing out your internal environment artificially. In the process of doing this, depending on your genes and the strength of the substance in addiction causation, the substance will cause a change in your gene expression in the cellular level (epigenetics) of your body and thus bind you to the substance (don't worry if you don't understand genetics, read on) – this is tantamount to the theory of evolution at a micro scale .

What is problematic is that it is not evident to the person when they are using, because they are enjoying it so much and you will often hear them say, "I'm only doing it because I love it, when it becomes a problem, I will stop", or something along those lines, and truly they do love it because, obviously, dopamine is being released throughout – everyone loves dopamine because everyone loves feeling good. It is unlikely for a person who does not have the gene that is specific for an alcohol-like substance to become addicted to it, as it is for someone who downright doesn't have genes for any substances at all but that person might just have genes that make him more susceptible to an addiction like food or gossip. Someone like me though, would have the propensity for addiction in many different spheres. Like I said, these genes vary, as well as the person's environment. I know a family of gossipers as well as a family of drug addicts.

"You have to reflect on yourself to discover who you really are" are the words of Mike Tyson in an interview with Joe Rogan when talking about his past and why he is so open about it, or as the ancient Kemets would say: know thyself. It was in this very interview that I instantly saw that Mr Tyson is an addict most probably as a result of his mother's addiction genes. This gene modification that is on a cellular level is heritable and on someone who has inherited this, there is no lag period whereby the habit is being formed and the genetic modification is occurring, basically you smoke now, you addicted now chief although on others, this lag period is significantly shortened over people who don't have this.

She would give him alcohol and marijuana as a child, in the hope that she could put him to sleep and this is where his addiction genes got activated.

Now what is interesting is that this disorder comes with obsession and being impulsive during the time of the modified genes and so it is no wonder that his trainer Cus D'Amato was able to redirect his flaw into a strength in boxing. The late great teacher would incite him to visualizing himself as a champion, this until he believed and got obsessed with the idea that he was the greatest in the world. His mentor took him away from the neighbourhood which he grew up in and which had been the perfect environment for these genes to express themselves – it is no wonder that by the age of 11 he had already started doing cocaine in this previous environment. Even becoming the youngest ever world heavyweight champion couldn't stop the code in his DNA from expression because even at the height of his career, he was abusing substances.

No wonder he has been "socially awkward" for most of his life, because that too is a product of the bittersweet gift, but then, society shuns those that are different and makes them feel crazy instead of embracing them. The shunning by society is what causes more imbalance in the internal environment of the individual because it is a traumatic experience, thereby increasing the substance use and strengthening the bondage. It was interesting to me how through the popular genetic tests done to trace ancestry, Tyson found that he is from Central Africa, which is the same region where Zulus and the rest of these relatives who now see each other as different tribes in Sub-Sahara , are said to have originated, or at least the last place which we had settled at before searching for greener pastures. When I found out about this, it made so much sense to me why he could throw a punch the way that he did, I could see that, no man, this comrade definitely has Zulu blood in him.

It is always so saddening to me when I hear that someone who had been suffering from depression committed suicide and people get so supportive, rally up behind the family and all the works but the same people will turn a blind eye when a drug addict is killed, because of the activities he engaged in, while he was trying to get his daily fix or even after he overdoses– these two people both couldn't control it and so they need the same amount of support and care. We need to learn to see things as they are and not how we (without any research or time taken to understand) choose to perceive them.

Day by day we have come to understand the human being more and more, thus some of the things that were seen as evil or totally wrong in the olden days, have come to being accepted and empathized upon by society today – culprits of uneducated damnations upon certain acts/groups are led at the forefront by some of the older institutions of metaphysics, as well as other influential groups that shape societal norms. The decisions, however, were probably the right way forward at the time when they were made, because, your analysis and judgement can only be as precise as your understanding. It is not enough to know, you must understand. It is the responsibility of us who live in the information age, to enhance these mechanical parts of our society by taking this car to service because the tyres are old, we are on the road and a thunderstorm is coming.

How does it feel being a substance addict? It is like living with someone else in your head, who suddenly takes control of the wheel and only wants you to eat food but somehow the more you eat, the hungrier you get and so you eat until you pass out. When you finally gain consciousness after a few hours, he then talks to you and asks, 'yey chief, did you eat before sleeping?', subsequently he takes over and leads you to the fridge. Everything in your life will then revolve around making sure that you find food so that he can be happy. Before you hit rock bottom, you will have the cute idea that it is you who wants the food and it is you who enjoys it, this because it is all happening in your mind, but you are wrong and you will soon find out that you are not in-charge of making these decisions. Some people are unlucky because they manage to avoid hitting rock bottom - this is a fatal skill which will shorten their lifespan dearly. I don't need to explain much on it because these days addiction is probably at the highest that it has ever been in human history as a result of the child prodigy that is social media. I've been asking myself these days as to when will a similar operation as the "SAY NO!" - that we got whilst still primary school children – be implemented to the youth of today but focused on social media rather than drugs, although I know that it won't work. What happens on this screen is synthetic environment that totally immerses you in it and everything that you see is designed to trigger addiction gene manipulation.

So how does one who is not inclined to genetics picture this modification? Well let's stay on the same wavelength as the analogy of the person who is constantly eating. So, the more the you eat, picture that it is your addiction genes that just gain weight and depending on your gene metabolism, you may have yours become obese instantly and another person will have theirs stay slim. What is sad is that once the person has his become obese, he can't make it lose the weight and the second person(Mr Hungry) then has a free pass to take over and demand you to eat in the manner which I have already explained – now it is no longer just you who wants to eat. Even when you reproduce, if the gene is passed on to your child, the child will inherit the gene as is. Once he grows up and tries out the substance with the same method of internal environment manipulation, for instance a depressant like alcohol, the poor child will be instantly KO'd and Mr Hungry (a fragment personality) will thus constantly be demanding the substance use from the child.

THE START

The Pygmalion Effect was coined after studies which show that the words which a teacher or authority figure utters as an expectation from an individual child, will become prophetic for that child's duration in the school; a child who is said to be a slow learner will become and remain a slow learner because of the psychological effect that is the Pygmalion. So a child who grew up in a household without his biological parents is surely at the mercy of the grown-ups who are his guardians: he is an easy target for childhood trauma -which Dr Gabor Mate points to as the trigger for addiction - and utterances such as "you're just like your father, you'll be a drunkard and will never amount to much", then it is only a matter of time before the puppeteer starts the show – in Ngoni language we say amazwi ayadala.

So where did it all start with the use? I was at the once Ndwandwe Kingdom where I knew I had to be ready for a fist fight at any point as soon as I left my family compound. Today brought something a little different because as I walked up the small trail towards the spot where I had a fight the week before, I heard someone scream my name as I passed one of the homesteads: A Ndwandwe relative of mine, who was probably older than my parents, called me to hangout with him. I obliged and was quite happy too because it was the festive season and I had not seen him for some time. There was music and some drinks were being served.

Ndwandwe: Zwide here, this is my favourite drink.

I took a can, opened it and had a sip – it was the most disgusting thing I had ever tasted. I put it down and shook my head.

Zwide: Ayngeke, this is horrible.

He laughed and pointed to a cider for me to try. It was much better than that poison he gave me and so I enjoyed the dumpie in their company. After I finished it, I stood up to take another from the table but I lost my footing and almost went head first through the table.

Ndwandwe: Hawu mshana! You are already drunk?

Zwide: No lutho, I am okay.

I hadn't finish it before we had to walk to the tavern in order to stock up some more. I was walking on borrowed legs. This is how I was to spend the remainder of my stay in the village, up until I had to go back to school. I resided in a quiet place during school periods and so I would only go out to visit my friends so that we could play video games, therefore, I didn't have much experience seeing people use substances, thus, I believed that people only drink when it is school holidays. I couldn't wait until I had to return back here but I was in for luck because I was to attend a high school where I would stay at a boarding house with teenagers from all walks of life and environments. As the year progressed those boys from townships became my favourites because they knew the places to go and the people to ask, for us to get what we wanted. I had been lied to all my life, had been told that drinking is a bad thing. From this time onwards, as my external environment abetted, I became a student on how to get it no matter what, other things didn't matter much.

This is why gaining influence of your internal environment is important for you to subdue the control which substance use has over you – your "internal environment" is in reference to your personal unconscious, as per Jung's model and I'm putting emphasis on the unconscious because once you get control of this, it will be easier to influence the conscious. Why so much emphasis on the internal environment? It is the neuroscientist Dr Joe Dispenza who eloquently explains how your thoughts have an effect on your bodily wellness and on your DNA expression. As such, you can improve your wellness through controlling your internal environment, you can edit your DNA expression through your internal environment. That which stands aloft your shoulders, is the most powerful tool that you possess, it separates you from all other living organisms.

The supply and use of "drugs" are an everyday thing in medicine but only a small number of people go on to full blown addiction after being given highly addictive substances like opioids. Why? The person's internal environment is told what the purpose of the medication is, and therefore this is like a cheat code such that he will not seek it after it has completed its purpose. Opioids are safely supplied to patients after surgery and they mostly don't seek the drug after it was administered correctly but should anyone of them then go experiment with heroin(opioid), the result in the number of those addicted would be totally different after just one use.

Interestingly enough though, before I got to the age where I was introduced to alcohol, we were made to fist fight with other boys in the village and I got to enjoy it for a time but when I became a fully initiated addict, I fell out of love with the act of fighting, it seemed pointless when one can just have a beer instead.

ENTROPY

It was a lively Friday at school; everyone was excited because at 18h00, the movie night was to start thus we couldn't wait for classes to end. I was on some other drift; I was closer to the older boys than ones my age, we were planning on how much we would need for the alcohol session because we knew that security would be handicapped at the boarding house since the screening was to be held at school. The four of us managed to come to an agreement and immediately after supper, we were to meet up at the rugby field right next to the forest in the spot where some boys smoke cigarettes during lunch break. It was so. It was dark by the beginning of the movie, so we comfortably started popping the liquor which had been sitting on the ice in the plastics. Menziwa was short, fast, ripped and was one of the best rugby players in the first team while, his best Mshiza, was skinny, tall, slow but was equally good as a backline player. My peer friend, Njomane, was tall, skinny and slow while I was short, fast and ripped – he was a player in my age group - so it was somewhat of a perfectly matched double date between the juniors and the senior players.

The short players were sitting on a bench and the tall ones were towering over us. It was quite fun spending time with the first team stars; they were telling us about the initiation into the team during their winter camp and they even showed us a couple of videos of the treatment of the initiates, by the first team veterans, in the name of "first team tradition". I realized then that the treatment they received in that camp is much worse than the one received by grade 8's from the hostel prefects when we first arrived into the boarding house. I must say though, at least their initiation was quick. After a few beers Menziwa then asked the future Bokkes

Menziwa: bafowethu, this is a model C school and we have all types of races in the same building but who here has one of the other races in their class?

Njomane: Me!

Menziwa: …And how come you are the only one?

Njomane: Obviously I had to do Afrikaans instead of Zulu as a first additional language.

Mshiza: *chuckles* You do Afrikaans instead of isiZulu? Aw Mr Njomane Van Der Merwe! *we all joined him with laughter*

Everything was grand up until our movie started; a vehicle with spotlights bombarded those awful things at us and it was immediately daytime again. I tried to stand up and my head felt like it weighed a ton but being the man that I was, I made the squat, the adrenaline was on an all-time high as Mshiza jumped over the bench like a springbok and beer bottles started spinning in the air. There was no choice but to get right into the forest and disappear into the shadows. One-by-one, people started disappearing and I heard hard thumping footsteps made by Menziwa far into the trees.

I was still on the same spot at this instance – every time I tried taking a step, I just fell hard. I came up with a plan; I was going to dive my way to freedom and so I did just that, I started jumping forward, landing on my chest then immediately standing up and diving again (it was painful but I was a man and so I took it like one). In what seemed like an 5 minutes later, I heard a voice behind me , "what are you doing ndoda?", so I stopped and turned - it was the school security guard and I was 2 metres away from the bench I had been sitting on. Njomane was standing with the security guards – I guessed that I was in a better state than he.

They started questioning me on where the others had run off to but it was evident that I was not saying a word, not because I was withholding information or was being disrespectful but because

I had suddenly lost ability to pronounce words. They quickly forgot about me and opted for Njomane. After a few phone calls and waiting, the shadows gave birth to Menziwa and Mshiza. Menziwa came back furious because according to him, our peace was disturbed. The security guards didn't flinch and opted to call for backup. Menziwa was shouting at everyone this whole time and I saw him rolling up his sleeves with my peripheral vision.

I was lying on the grass, trying to slither away like a worm but one of the polite gentlemen pointed a torch at me, so I played dead. Like clockwork, another bakkie arrived. Out came a huge coloured man who must've been 2 metres tall, with an equally big stomach, and the dwarfed Menziwa immediately became less aggressive although still defiant. We were put at the back of the van (they picked me up) and were told that the principal was to be called to speak to us.

The bakkie started moving towards the main gate where it stopped because the driver had to explain to his superior about us. I saw an opening: I immediately catapulted myself to the tar road, shoulder first, and because it had been more than an hour after the first attempt, I was more robust and I shot off from the line, I powered my way past a corner and into the pathway leading to the boarding house, I lifted my head and hit my stride, I could feel myself piercing through the wind, I was sure that my shadow could barely keep up with me, I entered the hostel main door and stomped up the stairs like Menziwa under the forest canopy: everything is a blur after that.

I woke up in the morning and realized that I was in the wrong dormitory and on the wrong bed. The owner must've been angry and retaliated, I thought, because the sheets as well as my pants were wet. No matter how hard I looked, I just couldn't find my slippers - all this didn't mean much to me because all I knew was that I needed a beer. This wasn't the first time I got inebriated however it surely was the beginning of the end of the beginning of my life at school. No wonder I was kindly asked to change schools at the end of the following year by the headmaster. One should always take responsibility for their actions but only this time around, I beg to differ.

We had had a school function two days before where there was alcohol being sold to the parents who had bought tickets. Purely by chance, Njomane and I were performing ballroom dancing on the night. He had told his "uncle" to buy a ticket and thus throughout the night we would slip away to the toilet and find his uncle with cans of beer waiting for us. The issue started a few days later, on a sunny Sunday after church, with the boys playing touch rugby and soccer on the top fields and the girls doing whatever it is that girls do, in the bottom field of the school. I don't remember who but someone must've known about the alcohol from two nights ago and where it was being kept. My hostel mates in my grade decided to go have a serious look at it for about an hour. After having the speedy look, we all headed back towards the sports field from the school buildings but we had to go back in groups of two to three in order to avoid attracting attention.

The Drunken master decided that he would go first, along with Inibu, no one objected because we all seemed okay and surely enough, they nonchalantly left, closely followed by others. I hadn't observed from all the angles and so Khabazela and I decided to leave last. From afar I could see that the Drunken master had already arrived and was sitting at the pavilion. I slowly and steadily made my way through the field towards the pavilion. As I kept my cool and looked, I could see the drunken master making his way down the stairs, towards the boarding house – he was walking like he had six legs, Khabazela couldn't contain himself from laughter, with his loud piercing voice. A parent couldn't have picked a worse day to visit their child because as soon as they made the turn towards the boarding house, the Drunken master attempted to do a hit and run on the vehicle but somehow fell right beside it after the initial hit. Inibu put his hands on his head and started crying. The Drunken master found his feet and ran inside the boarding house with a trail of vomit accompanying him. The parent just sat in the car in a frozen state for what seemed like a full thirty minutes.

All the boys in my grade were decisively gathered into the shower area and we were made to blow into the breathalyzer, although three of my peers had not been sightseeing with us and so they were easily let off because the boarding prefects couldn't smell anything dodgy in their breaths prior to them entering the court-room. When it was my turn, the needle went over the halfway point of the speedometer-like face of the instrument and I just knew that there was no explaining this. Somehow two of my comrades beat the test and were set free but the other four of us were booked. The drunken master wasn't even tested because he was asleep on the floor in a puddle of his own making. Khabazela blew and looked at the needle, then started swearing at everyone in the room, walked towards the master and kicked him.

I don't know how but the deputy principal, who was also the boarding house master, managed to turn this incident into a school offence instead of a hostel one. On the Monday, we were all called to the deputy's office for some explaining. The drunken master had called his uncle to speak for him. The three of them had a private meeting and it wasn't even ten minutes later that they came out of the office and he was a free man – we later learnt that his uncle was a lawyer. The rest of us were called into the office as a group and we represented ourselves. Zikode started telling his story and apparently he had been stopped by a group of older vagrant boys during his way back from the mall and they forced him to have two beers otherwise they would beat him up, "I tried telling them that I don't drink", he said, with a sombre look on his face. Second was Bheje, The Motorbike: the incident happened on a Sunday and so according to him, the reason why there was alcohol in his system was because he had been to church and there was a eucharist on that day, thus, there was wine that they were all made to drink as "the blood of Jesus". I looked at him and could see him shaking, then tears started flowing down his cheeks. He put his right hand over his chest and, with his classic stutter, pleaded that the deputy should call his pastor if he didn't believe him.

It was like someone had thrown a stun grenade in the room because everyone just sat there looking at him without the slightest movement. The deputy stopped him after a few minutes and told him that he could go. He then looked at me and asked me what my story was. I was honestly still shook from what I had just witnessed from Bheje and my mind stopped working completely, so I just said that I had asked one of the older day scholars to buy me beer at the mall. Khabazela must've been in a similar state because he also just admitted to being drunk on the day but I wasn't even listening by then because I was experiencing cognitive dissonance, asking myself whether Bheje was with us or was really at church drinking holy blood the previous day.

The system of signing for offences had already swallowed up most of us in our boys only Zulu class and it seemed that people in the Afrikaans classes were angels because barely any of them seemed to be getting warning letters compared to over half of my classmates. Even Njomane was hailed for his "good behaviour" in that group of angels. I don't remember anyone in the girl's classrooms being called up to receive a warning letter during assembly. From the first week in grade 8, our class teacher gave us a short moving address in his booming voice, cold blue eyes and square frame. We were the first group to be divided by both gender and language and so I couldn't understand at the time, how he could make such accurate predictions: was he a sangoma?

Mr Hills: HEY PUNKS! You lot, are the punks of the school! I'm telling you, I promise you, most of you here won't make it to the following grade. More than half of you are either going to fail or get expelled!

He then proceeded to sit down, lay back and read his newspaper and thus the Pygmalion effect was initiated on us.

One couldn't even ask for a rubber in class because we just knew that we were going to be made to sign for "talking in class", then when you try to explain, suddenly you are being made to sign for "refusing to sign".

Mr Hills: HEY PUNK! WOZA!

It felt as though you had someone looking over your shoulder at all times of the day – your shirt comes out of your pants when you are playing during break time and you will sign for that too. At least we got to practice our signatures though.

I too was then swallowed by the Punk system after receiving the blood of Jesus demerits. I received my 3rd and final warning letter, went to tribunal and got my hours of community service. What was interesting though was that during the tribunal when the Headmaster and the board members of the school were looking through my file, they kept praising me for my good marks and how I was playing lots of sport, even being in the leadership roles but they couldn't tell what exactly was my problem and so they asked me: unsurprisingly, I didn't know either. A comment on such a school is that it requires a particular type of learner with a particular personality trait, in this case it was for a conscientious agreeable pupil and so as soon as a creative person steps in, for instance, they are immediately branded as a bad apple as if one chooses their personality type. Nonetheless there were other much deeper factors at play and they were as systemic as their father who had departed in 1994.

From the first day of community service the DP was so happy, he was smiling for days, especially because he was the one instructing us to do what and where. On the first day of serving my service we all met outside his office as per instruction and we could hear him singing some RnB at the top of his voice. We were no more than ten, with most of the group being boys from my class, surprisingly. He told half the boys to pick up litter and other to sweep along the corridors. There were three of us left.

DP: AHHH! Zwide, Ndaba and Nkosi, follow me!...

he led us to the girls' toilets

DP: Zwide, you see these toilets? THEY MUST SHIIIIIINE! THEY

MUST SHIIIIINE! You hear me Ndaba?

Nonetheless, I didn't make it through the year, I was subtly given the boot.

During the December holidays I had to attend the SALGA Games which I had qualified for earlier on. I first saw him at athletics qualifications for our district – where he destroyed the competition - and he looked about ten years older than me although he was in the U16 and I was U15 at the time. We both qualified to represent our district and got to do training together at the nearby university, before heading to Pietermaritzburg for the meeting. We first shared a conversation after we were both in an excruciatingly long laugh which got worse every second. We had both been ridiculing the same thing; a fellow athlete arrived to training who was not there during trials but he had somehow qualified but that's not what tickled our tummies; the first thing I realised about Njini(engine) was that he was ripped like no human I had ever seen before, he was short and looked 20 years older than everyone else(the fact that he had some grey hair didn't help one bit), we got the opportunity to see him sprint with athletes in "his age group" and we couldn't believe how he just took off and became one with the wind , it was almost as if he was sprinting with his children. We named him Njini: The V12, and we made car noises every time it was his turn to run.

Makhathini had beer in his room and ,me being me, I just couldn't let my new pal have to endure all that drinking alone, I mean, he might get alcohol poisoning or something of that nature – these things happen to the best of us. It was at the time when our heads were already buzzing, after a few beers, that he whipped out a pack of cigarettes. He took one out and offered me one but I told him that I'm okay. He lit up his own and once it was halfway he offered me to have two pulls. What's two pulls anyway? I huffed and puffed. The next day we managed to pool money for more beers, and a pack of cigarettes which we would share because I had felt the day before how beer and cigarettes are just a match made in heaven.

This is basically how our two-week getaway went throughout its duration. Makhathini and I even met up a few times after the competition but not as often as we liked because he was actually from Jozi, it was a solid friendship nonetheless. A year later ,he was involved in a car accident whilst street racing drunk on his birthday, paramedics arrived to the scene and he asked that they start with his passenger(MJ) because he thought that he wasn't injured at all - according to MJ, at the funeral - so they did just that but unfortunately he died a few minutes later due to internal bleeding.

WHO IS THE MASTER?

I found myself having difficulty finding a new school and I couldn't understand why but I eventually got accepted in one of the last high schools in the south coast of KZN along the coastline. It was my first time going so far away from home and I took three taxi's before arriving at the small town before using the metre taxi that would lead me into the woods where the school was situated. For a second, I thought that I was in another world when I had arrived in the small town and decided to buy something to fill my stomach at a fast food franchise; I spoke to the cashier in Zulu and she just spoke in a tongue that made my hair stand – I really felt like I was on a different planet- because all my life I had been around English and Zulu speakers, and even the Afrikaans speakers would switch to English, as a "common tongue" but someone with my skin tone definitely speaks Zulu.

I then scanned her more fiercely after I had gained back my wits and it was strange to me how I couldn't tell by observing her, that she was a Xhosa. Wasn't she supposed to have a different skin tone or some other giveaway feature so that she could be easily distinguished as not Zulu?

As per weekend special, even at this new school, I couldn't help but find where the ethanol is most congested with no correlation. Probably 50% of the learners in the boarding house were new students and only about 10% of the school population are day scholars. We, the foreigners, stayed at the hostel and this is where we find this act: inebriation galore, the meeting and rubbing of shoulders between strangers is rife.

The boys seemed to have the wildest personalities I'd ever seen in my life and the young girls surprisingly seemed to be equal to them. After a few hours of mingling with the cool kids it was finally time for the champ to go to bed and have the half a litre of vodka – under the pillow - all to himself. See, the layout of the hostel was similar to how a traditional Ngoni homestead is planned out, with rondovels in a circular pattern all around the yard and there having to be an open space in the middle, in this case though there were interconnecting pathways inbetween and a centre garden with makeshift benches surrounding the tree and shrub garden. The girls' rondovels are at the bottom of the inclined circular format and the boys' are at the top of it, such that the man is as he should be in baNtu custom.

Scene 2 starts I go uphill and live to drink another day. Upon reaching the top of the hill I find a few of my newly found friends sitting under a tree as if they were sitting in the shade, only it was around 2 in the morning so this was a curious event but it was none of my business so I decided to pass them swiftly. one of them – Gagashe – wasn't having it, "Wola skhokho! Come have a few pulls, I will hold for you", so I swayingly came closer towards the pungent darkness and lowered my head towards the clenched fist with some cylindrical object inside and I inhaled two times then left as soon as I had arrived. I went into my room where I found my four roommates all inside, conversing and sober – I couldn't fathom how they could be sober and happy at the same time. As I walked inside, they all looked at me with glee and started asking for my opinion on which girl was the most good looking so that I would break the tie between them. With no hesitation, "Tgal bafwethu, anyone with eyes can see", and one side of the room erupted with glee and laughter. I went straight for my half of the double bunk. My bunk mate was Dj Gabz, a ladies man -well, at least according himself. Dj was a Xhosa and every time he opened his mouth to say something, I would just fail to hold my composure and would break out into unending laughter. What the hell had Gagashe given me? I was in tears by the time his grandmother called and – to solidify the stereotype of big boned people – he complained about the food not being to his liking at the hostel.

Dj Gabz: …ewe makhulu, hhay asitshi kakuhle apha.

I woke Gagashe up a few hours later because I wanted more of what he had given me the night before. I knew that I could never go back to the incomplete life that I previously lived.

The school grounds during break time would just be covered by a cloud of smoke such that you could barely see the person next to you – most of the smoke was not from the cigarettes however, but that didn't stop anyone from holding, whatever they were puffing on, like a cigarette. I didn't know a school could be run like this. It normally takes time for one to get fully addicted after the first initiation to an addictive substance however I already had the propensity even before I had my first drink, by now I could've inhaled and ingested anything I could get my hands on because my whole lifestyle revolved not being sober.

I was not aware that this was the cause of my whole personality totally changing because I figured that it was just a natural evolution as a teenager grows. When the addiction muscles are fully flexed and you are dependent, a new personality arises, Mr Hungry takes centre stage, while you fade away at the background. The new lad is strongest when a substance is available because that is when he would relax and stop being so contentious to everyone around him. My state of mind was such that I was only happy when I wasn't sober. I was now in a safe haven for addiction, the lack of disciplinary action by the school allowed for those who were already addicts to influence and teach those who weren't. Peer pressure was walking around with such bravado in this institution.

It was very difficult for us to get substances inside the hostel grounds because there was always security doing the rounds in and outside the fence but that didn't seem to stop us. Whenever there was to be alcohol bought, there would be a group of around three people who would collect monies from down the hill as well as up and then they would call a metre taxi which would be instructed not to go towards the gate but rather stay behind the trees, around the hostel ,and wait. The group would then jump over the fence and make sure not to get seen by anyone, this was very tricky and thus there would be spotters that made sure that everything ran smoothly. It was common for people to get caught, especially the inexperienced younger boys who didn't want to pay the fee that they were obligated to, upon making an order from the big boys.

During weekends, the authorities always knew that we were going to make a move but they just didn't know when in the day it was going to happen but as sure as night and day, a move was going to be made, therefore they would be constantly glancing towards us and we did the same to them, while puffing away at our "cigarettes". There was this one particular weekend where almost all the seniors jumped the fence and went down to town, including the girls. When we got to town it was as if there was a school day trip. We decided to collaborate and drink in the forest that was just behind the mall: We hadn't even been there an hour and there was a pair of policemen sprinting towards us screaming ,"DON'T MOVE, DON'T MOVE!" but a swarm made a run for it because most had illegal substances with them. I had a bad experience with running away from authorities the previous year, so I just gulped down the beer I had in my hand and stood there with some of the girls.

One of the police officers chased the ones who were running away and the other stood with us. We were questioned for a few minutes, then all our alcohol was sadly taken away and put inside the vans. We were taken to the police station. Upon arrival we were given some forms to fill in where we had to fill in our details and, obviously, we all filled in our real names and surnames. It was odd how I never saw them bring in our alcohol and somehow some of them knew two of the girls in our group – they started chatting and laughing about some experiences they had together. They let us go and took us back to town where we had to call the others who had ran away so that we could make another plan. I went into my pocket and took out the pack of weed that I had in my pocket so we could smoke while we waited.

Little did we know that there was going to be a minor problem on Monday. Afterschool when we were all tired and in need of some rest - after our hectic weekend and school - all the known smokers were called to the head office crew by crew. A few of us immediately noticed this and thus began the excruciating process of flushing our systems: each man had an empty 2 litre that they found, filled with water and downed like there was no tomorrow. I was only called to the office in the evening and was one of the last to be called, possibly because they were still not sure about me considering I was always participating in sport and doing quite well. I walked into the office and at the entrance was one of the girls I was with on Friday and she was making it rain all over her cheeks – no wonder the atmosphere in the room was so humid.

The principal acknowledged my presence and used a lit cigarette as a pointer to a chair for me to sit down while she exhaled the smoke. She was on the telephone speaking to a parent apparently, "yes, is this Mr Shamase? Yes, you are speaking to the principal at your daughter, Thobeka's school...I'm not well at all...well we found out that your daughter is smoking marijuana and we had had suspicions for some time now, we made her do a drug test which came back positive...yes...we are going to need you to fetch her as soon as possible because she is suspended for two weeks while we deliberate what is to follow...yes thank you, have a wonderful day...bye". The deputy principal walked in with Gagashe, carrying a small beaker with urine inside it, which they put on the principal's table – Gagashe glanced at me with his permanently red eyes and a face as if he were about to burst out in laughter. The deputy told me to follow him to the toilet and so I slowly dragged myself behind him because I knew that this was the end.

I was given a similar beaker and sure enough was told to turn towards the toilet and pee in it, this wasn't hard considering that my bladder was by now the size of a Jojo tank. I filled up the container and the deputy waited further while I put the full beaker aside and emptied my bladder for another minute. We went back to the office but along the way, we could hear the high-pitched voices of teenage girls, it went hand in hand with the singing of birds in the trees in this sea breeze infested afternoon. Right there and then I contemplated having a seizure that was going to go on until an ambulance was called but I decided against it, then I thought of Bheje and wished I had gone to church on Sunday because I had no problem being a Rastafarian for the remainder of my stay in this school.

I decided that I was going to say that I entered Thobeka's dormitory during the weekend while there was a cloud of smoke which smelt so awful and caused me to cough profusely. Gagashe was no longer around by the time we were back, the headmaster had a newly lit cigarette in hand. I sat down and waited for the tester to show my results while I played out, in my head, how shocked I would look. After what felt like an hour, the principal tilted her head downwards so as to look at me over her prescription glasses.

Principal: You may leave...

I stood up, put my right hand over my chest and opened my mouth wide open in dismay.

Zwide: ...but that's absurd, I've never touched the stuff in my life! It is probably because these girls had...

The boss lady wasn't having it, she cut my speech short with an demeaning retort.

Principal: I have no time for your stories, I still have to deal with these druggies here, now go back to hostel!

 She frantically lit up another cigarette. I Looked at her for a second and then I slowly walked towards the exit, with the expectation that I was being played for a fool, but my name was never called. I walked back towards the boarding house as the last sun rays of the day waved at me.

The event got me thinking that I wasn't going to last in the school nor did I want to continue there, so I wrote a visceral letter to my former school, requesting for them to take me back. I was unfortunate to get their reply which had good news in it, I thought. The reason why I made the request to them and not any other school was because they had had us believing that they were the best and every top university wanted their learners first. There were even blazers with colours for the achievers and so I truly believed that I needed that blazer, I needed to get my matric at their school in order for my life to be a success.

U-TURN

During the festive season I had to visit at my family headquarters. This is at the town where the royal palace is also situated, no wonder there are so many warriors and people with a deep sense of Zulu custom. The Zulu warrior way of raising children means that most don't know nothing but how to fight and so because there are hardly any wars anymore, some just end up as hitmen for a living, if not some low wage jobs because there is a general lack of exposure to anything else – if you are not a doctor, nurse or a teacher then you are most likely doomed for the rest of your life. Everyone knows where to find the hitmen and it is so easy to spot one because most of the time you just have to find the certain uniform at the taxi rank. Calling someone inkabi(hitman) is a common greeting.

The biggest blessing about growing up here is that you are pushed into fights by the older boys, from a young age - this is the first stage in becoming a warrior and gaining respect from members of the village but this is also how you learn to fight for what you want in life. One other thing that is highly common is the drinking of beer. Zulu beer is very critical. I always get excited when it's time to ukugiya (Zulu "dance") – this usually happens when the beer starts to hit the right spot – a lead singer will start a song bese kuyashuba endlini, kuchitheke ama salad. People smoke marijuana all over but it wasn't so common in my village, among the youth, now here I come with a bag full of the stuff and by now I'm smoking around 10 blunts a day – I was forever prancing on the clouds.

A close friend of mine decided to try it out while we were having some vodka that we dashed with ihlala (monkey orange fruit) because we couldn't afford any mixer : I was more than happy to supply him with his own blunt. It was as hot as northern KwaZulu gets, not to mention the dry air, we were drinking under the shade of the ihlala tree on the grazing fields. There were many bushes and shrubs around, including a thorny shrub right next to us, which we used as a stash place just in case some thirsty bastard were to come close and see our happy juice (we were having none of that).

Shandu lit up his herb and started hitting it while I blazed my own right next to him, the bottle was already at its shoulders by now so we had been sipping from our cups diligently. He stood up after hitting a few pulls because he was coughing profusely. He decided that he needed something to clear his throat so he thought he should pour some more holy water into his glass and thus he moved towards the thorny figure - with the biggest smile that I'd ever seen on him. As he bent over, the ground must've opened up because he went right into the thorns in a spectacular fashion, me being myself, I couldn't stop the tears from running down my cheeks and got paralyzed with laughter. Honestly speaking, booze and weed don't go well together, if you really have to light one up, better light it up before you start drinking but if you do the opposite it will only lead to an unnatural disaster.

There's nothing wrong with having a beer whilst getting high, the problem is when you do it on a regular basis because this will have a devastating snowball effect on your body and mind, add a third substance (e.g nicotine) to the field and you've basically irritated a snake which it is hiding in its burrow. A substance alone, used correctly, is not bad at all, drugs are actually beneficial to us most of the time but abuse them and they will abuse you too, combine them and they will start gnawing you up piece by piece. It also goes without saying that although Shandu is the one who asked for the plant, I am the one who unwittingly persuaded him to want to try it out - the fact that he was with me a lot, combined with the alcohol in his system, it was just a matter of time before he wanted to try : people who use these substances already know that you are curious, all they do is just push you in the direction and nothing makes them happier than seeing a new member to the family.

Returning to a school had previously chased me away was quite dilemmatic: My original friends treated me different because I was also different and I felt as if eyes were on me in the first few days, even from people who I wished to avoid. The teachers were obviously briefed about such a legendary learner thus one mistake, one signature. I was put in the top Zulu class because despite the drama I went through, I had decent marks from the school in the woods. The class of the top learners only had girls and one other boy – whom they picked to be the headboy. In order to maintain my habits, I decided to sell some Nice-Nice at school. I had learned the art of selling when I was South Coast at the boarding house because the most feared learner didn't use any substances but was keen on making a profit from us, he therefore bought stock and hired some of us to push it for him.

The worst thing that could've happened actually happened in my first week back: a party where we got inebriated to a point that we thought that we could bully the police. They came on cue when it was most fun and decided to ruin our happiness. We started pushing them to leave right away, one policeman gave my mate the most extreme slap I had ever seen, this was followed by a segue to an adrenalin fuelled sprint by him and it was then that we too actually agreed that ending the party was a good idea. SAPS should teach all South African track event athletics coaches how to slap like that. It was not long after that I realized that returning was the biggest mistake I could have ever made because I didn't have much of it the first time but now I completely lost my peace of mind, especially whilst on the school premises. Being in the presence of people, who don't want you around, is never wise. That which is in the past, should stay there, because it has already served its purpose in your life. This eye opening realization was the catalyst for my new found depression, and as a result, I inevitably swam at the deepest end of the substance abuse swimming pool: evidence was how I almost always carried some hard liquor either in my school blazer or in my bag if it was the big bottle.

I luckily got chased away again at the end of the year. It was during the final exams of the year and my grade was not writing on the day and so we decided to have a chill session where we did what we do best. During the session, when the liquor was in our systems, we realized that there were no girls with us. Zikode and I (yes, he had somehow survived this whole time) decided to go call them at the boarding house. As soon as we entered the school premises, just after the boarding entrance, we saw the school taxi racing across the field towards the boarding houses but we thought nothing of it until it swerved towards us and out came the DP and his sidekick. Zikode swiftly put the dumpie in his crotch and I dropped my styrofoam cup but it was too little too late. The Dp's face was glowing inside the taxi as they took us to his office.

DP: YAAAH ZWIDE! I got you! You thought you had us all fooled. Huh!

We were made to blow on a similar breathalyzer as the one from the boarding house toilets two years back and by now we had learnt the trick that was used by those who avoided trouble and so the needle didn't move an inch on both of us.

DP: No no, this can't be. You still think you're clever huh? Wait here I'm going to buy a different tester.

He came back some time later with some balloon-like device which we had to fill with air and that's when the sun set on us.

Zikode somehow survived this event again and managed to finish at the school although he was banned from taking part in school extracurricular activities.

FACTORS WHICH ESCALATE AND WORSEN

It couldn't have been two days after my arrival to the big city: it was sunny as always, with the temperature around 25 degrees Celsius in the coast. I was having a beer in a local drinking spot, crushing some herb beneath the table as if I were hiding it, but really wasn't. 2$6 saw and approached me. I looked up in bewilderment as I was not expecting a familiar face. We spent time together one weekend when the rebels from South Coast and I decided to party in Durban because Mpelu grew up here and so he wanted us to experience his "hood". I was surprized that I recognized him because I was being carried for most of the three days that we were here. He was part of the woonga epidemic that swept the country in the late 00's and early 10's and so I knew that he was expecting me to give him a few rands.

I sat him down and caught up with him while I finished rolling and put my pipe in my pocket. He told me the story of how a member of the 26 gang recruited him to become a woonga dealer. Through exposure and time, he ended up trying it just for the heck of it, but he didn't know that by this experiment, he was actually signing over his soul to a higher being. You can tell that he has intellectual prowess whenever he has to make up a story as to why he needs money from his victim : "ey gogo wami I arrived in Durban two weeks ago with the hope of being admitted into the University of KwaZulu Natal, luckily I was able to enrol into pharmacy but the problem is that I don't have NSFAS yet and I don't have any parents and thus I have to bath and sleep in the school toilets until I can get funding, If I could only just get R100 so that I am able to at least have something going towards my stomach - I would appreciate it and the Lord will bless you".

Let's have a better understanding of this external environment before we continue. When it comes to the hard drugs like ecstasy, cocaine and woonga, those who deal in these are almost always foreign national in the black African communities and the CBDs – this differs in communities dominated by other racial groups but I'm focusing specifically on the black African because that's what I know first-hand. As per what I could decipher during my time and still see today, most immigrants from neighbouring countries are here because of economic reasons etcetera etcetera, I know you just want the cream so here it is: most of them are just employees that do the dirty work of dealing. They are the best candidates because they are not known personally by the community members nor do we had good communication because of the language barrier, unlike me whereby it would be easy to track that I'm so and so's child who stays at such and such place because it is a small country and we are all connected in one way or the other. Secondly, they are desperate to make a living and would do anything to survive.

The citizens of this country who engage in the dealing of hard drugs in the streets (in the black African community) are normally those that are part of the gangs. Our history has taught us that the best way to overcome adversity is through reconciliation, sharing each other's spaces and through the understanding of one another. In order to induce unity and decrease the amount of substance addiction at the same time, through mass internal environment manipulation, I realized that firstly, there is no reason why examination question papers are written in both English and Afrikaans only when native speakers of such combined amount to only 10% of the population – There needs to also be an African language as a choice. I am adamant about this especially because I've attended both multiracial(previously only white) and African schools(government) which we are still going to get to later; it was very common for me to come across a fellow pupil ,at the African school, who was in need of help with their school work and I would explain to them vehemently in depth about their problem but still umuNtu is still confused. It would only be after I was agitated and ready to give up that I finally just translate it as best I could, using a sentence or two into isiZulu, and like magic umuNtu says "ohhhhhhhhhh".

It is ridiculous how even some of the teachers in these predominantly African schools are some of the most intelligent people you have ever met but their biggest hindrance in life has been their lack of eloquence and grasp of the English tongue, thus probably preventing some of them from fulfilling their calling – he ends up teaching during the day and immediately going to the tavern after work to drink until they have to carry him home because his internal environment has been gravely imbalanced by these systemic chains. It becomes a never ending cycle because his learners will also have a hard time grasping the foreign tongue - even English had to be taught in isiZulu in order for the teacher to have a hope of her learners passing - and if they do enough to get into university, it is here that they find lecturers with foreign accents and different pronunciations of English from what they are used to. It is because of such that I believe that inclusion of an African language will have a multiplier effect on societal healing. Language determines how you think but more importantly, language determines what you can think.

We could choose the most commonly spoken and well known language in our country- like how countries further north have integrated Swahili, not surprisingly though because that is the most widely spoken language in our continent - this will prevent time wastage on debates and politicking for over half a century before anything happens, just like how we already have waited that long in matters like those of the freedom charter. We then translate academic textbooks from what is in the foreign tongue into the endemic, in the same way that the bible was.

Now that we have completed this step, we will then change Eurocentric methods into structures that also resonate with an African mind, and African environment or have a combination because we are a rainbow nation after all – there is no reason why grade 1 learners are taught that 'i' is for igloo, when they are introduced to the alphabet. This will also be a solution to the masses of our people who don't have the financial luxury to afford "racially integrated" schools and thus struggle under the English language even today.

It wasn't long after, that I seemingly went on the same path as 2$6. Naturally, I had to ask him to show me around the area such that I am familiar with my surroundings as well as with the crew who I only remember flashes of during the times when I was conscious the last time I was here. The gang hanged out opposite the mall area where there is a chain of rental buildings and smaller shops that are usually owned by Nigerians and Bangladeshi, If not Indian people. We were permanently outside a Nigerian owned tuckshop that had a sister store right next to it, which was a butchery. The funny thing with the sister side is that there was never any meat that you could see nor any customers, besides a few police officers that would be on the regular on Fridays. What was more odd though was that only one officer would exit the vehicle, enter the butchery and he would seemingly come out within ten minutes with nothing in hand – I was amazed at how fast the service was as well as how fast the officer would finish his supposed meal. In the evening, the boss would arrive – normally with his black German vehicle.

Everyone would be so happy to see the boss and they would cater to telling him funny stories, but he would just smirk a little and then tell us about how big he is, it would always start with , "You see me my friendo, I'm telling you…" ,then he would tell us about the car which he is thinking of buying or the 8 bedroom house he apparently has at Umhlanga Rocks. The crew members had refused to work for the boss because of his conditions, so they would make money by working as taxi conductors unofficially and pickpocketers officially – the blackberry smartphones of the university students were never safe, especially ones of the American wannabes with sagging pants.

I think that the reason why they targeted the wannabes was because they instinctively knew that these kids had their heads somewhere in the Bronx, recording a mixtape with OG Shootout, not in South Africa eDubane – this made them an easy target because they are not aware of their surroundings. The taxi route would be down the CBD using West street until we reached South Beach – where usually one of the members would quickly jump off – then we would come back on Smith street, around the Durban University of Technology until we reached our chill spot where there would be a change in the conductor every once in a while until everyone gets a chance to go at least once or twice.

2$6 took me with whenever it was his chance at first and it was fascinating how all the taxis were so brightly coloured with all these beautiful designs and customizations on the outside as well as inside the minibus, don't get me started on the music because all of them were so loud such that you could hardly hear the person sitting next to you shout. Whenever the conductor wanted to stop the vehicle in order for a passenger to get on or off, he had to bang the outside of the door such that the quantum sounds like how an empty vessel would. Like clockwork, whenever we got south, one of the members would jump off and allow us to go on without him, but soon after we got back to the chill spot, he would suddenly jump off another vehicle within 5 minutes of our arrival and then the most amazing thing would happen : all the crew members would immediately surround him and receive their daily bread in a eucharist-like manner.

I eventually decided to try the pill after I had initially slammed them for doing "drugs". I would look at them and shake my head, but they would seemingly be oblivious to my remarks and proceed to enjoy themselves. Again, overtime as I spent more and more time with them, I slowly got accustomed to what was happening and my view on the usage also evolved because this became a normal thing to me just as it was to them : this is why there is a saying that goes, "show me your friends and I will tell you who you are", with time, the habits and energies of the people you spent most of your time with, will seep into you without you even realizing it, it is not something you can control, the best way to prevent it is by not spending time with energies which you see as being negative.

It was a boring Friday during our hour long school lunch break and I had just received my monthly allowance for groceries: as usual I was outside the G's shop, having one or two puffs and one of my companions had been a dealer for a week or so after being recruited by some coloureds whom he told me were his childhood friends. I asked him to give me one – it wasn't a big deal because they always do it and seem to be always enjoying, so why not? Twenty minutes passed by and I couldn't feel a thing so I started complaining to Meshenti because it was obvious that he was selling me a placebo; I got angry and went back to class but I told him that one way or another, he was going to pay back my money. I got to class a few minutes late - but it didn't matter much in this school, even if it was the principal who was teaching in this period- and I immediately sat down to write the notes on the board which were already close to the bottom of the board. I got to work, ferociously, with the pen held tightly by my three fingers, to an extent that I felt that I was going to snap it. I was not even halfway on my first page and suddenly I felt a rhythm within me, I frowned and my lips tighten, I started nodding my head, the chalk board became blurry all of a sudden so I jumped up from my chair and stomped my way towards the headmaster.

Zwide: sorry meneer, I'm not feeling well, can I please run to the toilet.

I then frowned while clenching my fist as well as my jaws, I moved my head side to side rhythmically but slowly, I lowered my body as if I were bowing and then I slowly came back up whilst my shoulders were rotating (I did not know this at the time but I had just came up with my signature dance move). The headmaster looked at me worryingly and being the Life science teacher that he was, diagnosed me as having a tummy bug so he told me to rush before I changed the smell of the room, so I swiftly moved out while doing my dance. I got to the toilet, put on my earphones and listened to house music until the final school bell. The party didn't end just then: obviously I had to go salute Meshenti for being the man of the match.

This was when the storm had just started because now I was having a cocktail of four different substances at once and they somehow worked so well together : I would start off with some herb just so I could plan out my day and get my creative juices flowing, this would be followed by a few drinks while waiting for a chance to work , after imbibing ethanol for a while I would feel sleepy and that would be the queue for me to talk to Meshenti if he were around or immediately get on a taxi towards South Beach – aka Lagos - and this is where I would talk to one of the G's and get ecstasy so that I would feel like a new man within thirty minutes.

I hadn't been able to stomach the act as of yet – I had a grudge because they had cheated me out of my grocery money early on after 2$6 introduced me to them - and so I would watch in dismay as some kid would invite the dogs to bite, after he said something like, "Ey Yo! Wadup dawg?". As soon as I could feel the effect of the pill, I would suddenly feel the need for some music and something to chew on and thus I would buy gum, hop on a quantum and get engulfed by the intense frequencies that were bouncing around inside it , with the only disturbance being the loud bang on the door and the signature , "Yahamba mfowethu?". I would spend an hour or two in the taxi, moving up and down the CBD repeatedly without having to pay because I am friends with the conductor and with the view I got here, I could see that the different drivers normally had a frown on their faces, would be chewing gum non-stop and moving their heads from side to side rhythmically.

Night would come and allow us to hit the club where the dance floor is where the fingers of my comrades would suddenly get longer and stickier, and there would be a lot of bumping into other Durbanites. Besides the dance floor shenanigans, what really brought us into one of the clubs was the warmth that was inside because it went very well with one particular substance that was in our blood for most of the night. Every thirty minutes or so we would go chill outside - to avoid overheating - opposite the road with the others who didn't want to enter on that particular night and it was usually quite a significant number : this is where all the smoking, snorting, selling and pill popping would happen.

Once we got outside, this is when people would suddenly reveal smartphones that they now had but hadn't walked in the club with and this was always so fascinating to me but it would at times get very hectic: immediately as we walked outside one time, a tall bloke with two of his friends tried stopping Meshenti but he was swift and shot away in a devastatingly fast sprint towards the opposite pavement - where there was unfortunately only three of us comrades– and he grinded right up the road as if he were going to detour and swerve towards the Workshop Mall.

I do not know how and where they came from but there was a whole athletics squad behind him and they were up to the task at hand, all we could do was jog behind them so we could see where all this was going. It was not even 400m up the road that they caught him and gave him the beating of his life: the tall bloke at one point picked him up and threw him in the air like a sack of potatoes in a warehouse, while the hyenas didn't waste time getting on him to tear him limb from limb till the lion could no longer roar anymore and the only sound that came from him was his body taking the blows from the death squad. 2$6 then shouted,

2$6: don't kill him, there's a street camera above you!

A few of them realized this and disciplined the rest of the clan; the giant took his phone from Meshenti's pockets and left with his clan of hyenas as they revisited and laughed about the whole experience. 2$6 went to Meshenti and asked him, "ubuwenzani nawe ungajimile?". It only hit me on this day that I was not really friends with these people and 2$6 was actually feeding me to the dogs. When you are always high or drunk and things are dry on a particular day, you end up taking whatever is available to you just so you can suppress any cravings that you might have and so by now I was fully ready and willing to do anything, even to accompany them on their trips, after clubbing, that they took to the tourist hotspots in South Beach because let's face it, none of us were ever sleepy.

Somehow this incident must've wiped the fog on my window a little: I was trapped though, and I knew it. Having this habit was destroying my health and I was always tired because of no sleep and lack of nutrition, it got to a point whereby my speech was slowing down and I sounded like a tape on slow motion. I developed a horrible paranoia. I never really had any food in my flat and would at times steal a few coins from my roommate's schoolbag so that I could at least have a vetkoek because I had inhaled, swallowed or imbibed all the money that I had received from home. It all happened as if at once; I was harvesting the fruit from the tree which I sown and nurtured throughout its vegetative and fruiting stages. I could hardly concentrate in class and was always so forgetful – the cream was when I would be talking to someone and would forget what I was trying to say halfway in a sentence, then I would try to act as if nothing happened and switch to another subject swiftly.

Judgement day came on warm night with clear skies when I went back to my flat, drunk on Russian vodka and a deep paranoia, climbed the stairs to the rooftop, stood alone at the edge and looked down…"it will only take a few seconds", I thought, "…no one will remember me if I do it anyway…",",…I have no reason to continue with this life, it's only full of pain and tears, then I will die anyway…", "…no one even loves me, no one cares for me…",I couldn't do it, something in me said that this is not it. I had to clearly define for myself what I want out of this life: I wanted to be free. I envisaged what freedom was for me and how I was going to get it. I promised myself that anytime I felt like the road I was on was no longer leading me to my freedom as I envisage it, then I would have to make a U-turn no matter what the cost – be it reputation or relationship because I figured that nothing could possibly get worse than right now. I saw it in my head and then I slowly retreated from my endeavour and went to bed.

I was depressed beyond measure and the combination with addiction was eating me up, literally, from the inside out. Around this time, I got a chance to see my weight and I had lost about 15kg from the time of the froggy jumps until now. I continued carrying a nip of vodka to school, every day that my pockets would allow.

I really don't understand how people bear the city for so long, with an external environment which is so synthetic. It's probably the air being constantly compressed as the vehicles approach and then the dispersion as the vehicle goes past, causing a constant whooshing sound in the CBD 24/7, which causes the imbalance in internal environment. No wonder so many people have lost their minds here and end up jumping from the top of the buildings to their demise like Kratos on the Bluffs. No wonder it is here that the hardest drugs are taken. What is worse is how these tall buildings are like what you see at the harbour with its stacked up square containers, then there is us inside like the cargo that we are. I'm quite certain that the lack of flora and fauna has something to do with it, but it is most definitely the combination of all of these that is so uncivilised.

My matric June exams came. The first examination was to be mathematics Paper 1 and I studied for a whole two days, solving x left right and centre papa. On the morning of the exam I was amped, I had a few blunts and vodka just to calm my nerves, then came time for me to enter the exam room: I filled in my answer script with my details neatly and waited for my question paper.

As soon as we were given and told to start reading, I scanned the paper thoroughly and thought that this was going to be okay because I didn't see anything which I had not seen before. We were told to start writing after the 10 minutes reading time which was set for the 2-hour paper. I filled in the question number on my script, '1.1.1…' I didn't know what to do actually, so I went to 1.1.2

but that question started with "hence" and I immediately knew that I was under siege so I skipped question 1 and looked at question 2, then 3 and then I glanced at the invigilator who locked eyes with me and pointed at my script. It must have been less than 10 minutes in when I stood up and handed in my empty script.

The snowball effect of substance abuse and environmental torture was like intellectual anaesthesia. The invigilator was my Geography teacher and she asked what the problem was but I only shrugged, then she was taken aback by the stench of alcohol. She asked me why I was drunk, I told her to leave me alone and I ran outside the pile of containers. I only went back there once again just to satisfy myself of the situation. I called home and told them that I couldn't do it anymore and I wanted to come back. I thought that it could only be up from here on although the slope was still flat.

ALIGNMENT

I got home and stayed sober through self-isolation for around 8 months. During the period, I got into the act of extirpating out the person who I was before I got back home. I knew that I had to literally become someone else and this can only be accomplished by being alone for an extended period of time. My mother took some convincing before she agreed to take me to a rehabilitation centre (I might have shed a tear or two) because she had asked me to go there on two previous occasions and I had utterly and despicably refused.

I originally couldn't fathom the idea of rehab because of the stigma that came along with it. What is crucial about taking the decision to go for treatment is that you should never go there if that is not what you truly desire, I made the request because I could see that I had put myself in the middle of a warzone but I didn't even have a knife, so I had to call for reinforcements to come drag me away. Rehab was only a matter of three weeks long, but it truly did change my life because it equipped me with the necessary weaponry needed to fight back, but most important was the first education on addiction which I had ever received, because that gave me answers to some of the most profound questions which I had about myself - like what the hell is wrong with me ?

My mother works in a very isolated quiet work village, thus the community we reside at is mostly quiet during the day, with hardly any unemployed people besides the few pupils who stay with their parents. I highly recommend that you first isolate yourself the first time you try controlling the hungry person within, if you want to quit, especially during the first few months because you are still very much vulnerable at this point.

I spent a lot of time in my room reflecting and envisaging what I want out of this life that I have been blessed with and I honestly didn't know what I wanted in the long run but I knew that I had to go back to school seeing as I didn't come from a rich family, had no skills, ideas and nor any connections. By chance I came across an interview, on Youtube, of Anthony T. Browder where he teaches about the history of black Africans, where he has evidence that suggests that the ancient Egyptians (Kemets) were black Africans who originated from south of the Sahara(before their lands were colonized by the Assyrians, Greeks, Persians, Romans and then the Arabs , how all these glorified Greek scholars- like Aristotle, Plato and Pythagorus – mostly just regurgitated what they studied in Egypt (George G.M James in Stolen Legacy) .

As time progressed over the years, I read further and discovered writings on the great city of Benin, Timbuktu, Great Zimbabwe but the initial knowledge gave me the confidence to look back at history in my most recent line of decent and the rest is history. I had been previously taught, directly and indirectly especially because this ideology has become synonymous with our culture as Southern Africans, that we were just savages before Europeans came to "save us" and they then "civilized us", that my culture and people were inferior and my ancestors demonic, that we hadn't accomplished anything nor contributed to mankind as the "dark continent" but now I knew that we actually originated everything and we are worthy – This was a covidous point in my life because it shifted my psyche in ways that will continue to manifest in the times to come.

I decided that when I get back to school I would have to pass with flying colours so that I could get a bursary which would give me the mobility to direct myself and so that the time I had wasted would seem insignificant when put against what this African has accomplished – I didn't know how I was going to go by this but I truly believed that I could do it because I have done more in my past lives. I kept a dark secret from myself - which would later lead to a relapse - and I stored it in the shadow of my consciousness.

My goal was set -I didn't tell anyone- and so I then decided to make sure that my mind was fit enough, mind you, I had not fully recovered it because my personality was still altered and I still had the cognitive ability of a six year old, although better than just before I went into rehab. I was a big fan of Dwayne Carter who was very influential at the time and who claimed that he worked every single day hence he was so successful, therefore that was my starting point.

I decided to learn and develop a new skill by mirroring him and this challenged my brain such that it activated parts which were asleep. I started writing every single day, mostly lyrics which were idiosyncratically similar to those of Mr Carter and short stories which I would enjoy reading. The stories were inspired by the dislike of those novels from English class that I thought took the fun right out of reading for me and would have me asleep after just one paragraph. Sometimes I would feel inspired and would write for hours on end and then other times I would dread even thinking about it – but I would do it anyway. It ended up happening automatically and I wouldn't be able to sleep peacefully if I went to bed without at least writing a page – this is the same thing that would happen previously whenever I tried going to bed without using an illegal substance – and now it got to a point where I would get an idea in my head and then get the urge to quickly go jot it down before I lost it.

We were taught how to meditate at the rehabilitation centre (I really enjoyed it) and through deep meditation one day, something hit me... I am not my body but I am the person inside, who just happens to reside in this vessel of meat - I took my new approach with both hands and ran with it in order to force myself to write even when my body and mind said no. It was then easier for me to do tasks whatever it might be; every time I had to write but felt uneasy about it, I would just remind myself that I am the master of this body and it will do whatever I tell it to, whether it likes it or not. Every day I would visualize the life that I wanted to lead and through meditation it was easy to focus all my being to this dream. Writing then became a habit through time, it was getting hard to find space to write on in the workbooks that I had.

There was a television show called Brain Games that I took an interest in and it influenced me into gaining my memory back and developing it further than it ever was before; I would also download memory games on my cellphone and would spend a lot of my time playing, if I wasn't writing. The most important thing which I gained from the show was seeing people who could memorize the order of the cards in their deck in a matter of minutes, - they taught us how they did this - it was this skill which I would later synchronize with my studying. With time I slowly regained my concentration and memory, I would actually get surprised and laugh at myself whenever I regained a portion of myself that I had lost due to my past activities: it's funny because during my run, I didn't realize how much I had changed and how little of me was left. I realized that the world as I knew it was totally different as from now on.

Everyone who I thought I knew switched up on me, friends were not picking up my calls, girls were not even looking my way anymore and some family members were spreading damning rumours – it seemed like I was somewhat excommunicated from society. I developed a general dislike for other people as well as an anger which was like poison to my soul. Whenever I would feel bad about my unfortunate predicament, I would just visualize the life I wanted to lead in the future, and this would then give me the strength to pick up my pen and go Shakespeare on the pages.

After a few months of locking myself in the house, I felt ready to step outside into the real world. The rehab centre taught us to stay away from friends whom we used to do go wild with and so I did just that and started going to church after an elder church leader approached me and had a conversation with me. I thought that it couldn't hurt to say yes. Additionally, to feeling that I should give it a chance, I thought that spending time around people would help me with my withdrawal symptoms. I was raised in a church going family and every Sunday it was in church where you would find me, even Sunday school I was there. I would always spend my time listening attentively and observing the speaker, the crowd, as well as what was being said. It is quite evident how spiritual organizations like those of Christianity, African Spirituality and Islam are crucial for society to function, they are at the cornerstone of hope, metaphysical fundamentals, discipline and faith, for many-a-people throughout the world. A life without purpose is no life at all and this too is a gift that some receive in these various spiritual families, others don't even need to see a psychologist because they get their psychological healing in these organizations. What works for one person is not necessarily what is good for another, therefore, just like Warren Buffett and the trees in the forest, it is in our diversity that we are rich.

The day that I was invited was in the first week of the new year, everything looked splendid in this college hall with its intricate decorations and the atmosphere was as if we are already halfway to heaven. The head of the church spoke with his hoarse voice and blessed us with his words – I could see why he has so many followers. When he was done preaching, he then proceeded to show us the vision of the church in the church screens: this was a humongous building and looked quite university-like. He revealed the amount of money that was raised the previous year, and which amounted to 65 million – the crowd went wild. He then went on to reassure them that the vision will be manifested, all they need to do is to "plant your seed". The band started singing in the most angelic and ear tickling manner. He took out an envelope from his pocket, put it in the basket in front of him and shouted,

Leader: PLANT YOUR SEED!

A whole squad of people stood up with their envelopes and headed towards the front, this continued for around 10 minutes with the choir showering us with sweet melodies. The choir then lowered their harmony until an eventual stop and then they sat down as the number of people going to the front declined. The Apostle now started an anecdote. He told us about a young incredible worshipper of the lord and showed slides on the projector. The family of this young man were not believers at first but rather followed the cultural and spiritual beliefs of baNtu peoples. The apostle told us, with images showing in the background, how he and his team were able to mould this young man as well as his family such that the "demons" that once ruled over them have been cast aside, all the baNtu spiritual possessions were removed from the homestead and then a video started where the young boy from primary school is shouting the contents of the bible to his fellow learners during morning prayer at his school. The crowd went wild again and shouted to the heavens, giving Him all the glory.

I felt so uneasy as I looked around. I waited for the tithe receiving bags – which were now being circulated – to reach me and I dropped all my net worth at that point in time: R2. I appreciated them for opening my eyes. I did not see at the time however, that one of the keys to beat my problem indefinitely lay in spirituality because it is in this that you can maintain power over the internal environment even if the external environment would change to being detrimental to your internal balance. It was only after I had relapsed again that I found God in myself and this gave me the strength to subdue it without external intervention.

I needed to gain some mass back, so I started going to a nearby gym where I eventually found a gym partner, named Kyle, who made everything a lot easier although I soon found out that gaining weight, for me, is harder than losing it. I would normally go in the evening when it was full, and on my walk there I noticed some kids – they ranged from 6 to 12 years old - that would always be playing at the nearby park. I eventually approached them and asked if they would be interested in me teaching them how to play rugby, one thing led to another and now I would be playing touch rugby with them as soon as they came back from school until Kyle past by with his green golf 1, then my warmup session would be over. I was finally finding a balance in my life but there was still that hole inside me, I was not happy at all. I thought that it would subside overtime but no, Mr Hungry was upset. During the day, whilst waiting for the kids to get back from school, I then started to spend my time at the local bar which I used to drink at before. I would buy cooldrink and chat with the barman all day, he would always ask me why I stopped so I eventually told him but I could see that he wasn't particularly happy about it – abusers are never happy if they see that you have quit, it gets under their skin because it reminds them of what they are going through inside. Honestly, the sober life wasn't doing it for me physiologically and psychologically. I couldn't understand what was going on because I thought that I had been cured of my problem. I felt like a kid that had just got his sweets taken away from him. There is no cure.

STAYING SOBER

I have experienced a village where most people make a living off of the cultivation of marijuana, I thus knew from early on how there are many economic opportunities in the marijuana trade – to them insango is just an ancient herb that the community has used and sown for centuries, and which used to be an honest source of income but today they get arrested for. As the Ngoni saying goes, a piece of meat got snatched from their mouths. What is quite perplexing to me is how the plant got criminalized by the Americans about a century ago but today one of their most profitable legally sold strains is a South African landrace sativa called Durban poison, in the USA. South Africa has the perfect climate for the cultivation of the crop, so it is no wonder that we have so many unique varieties that have developed over time; the Durban poison cultivar is just one of many varieties that is found on the streets.

We need such initiatives now more than ever especially with the worst employment rate our country has experienced in modern history. With my experience and everywhere I have been in the country to this day, a merchant is never more than 5km from wherever you are. No wonder a large portion of children begin using it as early as in primary school. These merchants don't care about the age of the buyer. Retail legalization and regulation could add a much needed dimension because then users would be able to buy a product that they can trace its origins and get know exactly what they are getting. Currently you never know what you are getting and some people fall victim to criminals which spray methylated spirits to the harvest in order to give a unique high, others lace ready-made joints with heroin inside and the result is initiates to the highly addictive drug, creating lifelong customers

- according to what I learned at SANCA, less than 20% of people who go to rehab with a heroin addiction are able to beat it, they almost always relapse.

I got to see the effects first-hand when we got a chance to go out to town for the first time since entering the rehab centre. We got given a few hours in the last weekend so that we could trial our reintroduction to society. I went out with someone whom I had gotten close to during my stay and his name was Mageba. This was his third time at a rehabilitation centre and he had been telling me about how this one was the best that he had been to because in the government run ones he never got any medication to help with the excruciating pain that woonga smokers experience as withdrawal symptoms just a few hours after they last smoked. We walked around the CBD and I passed by Berea to greet some of my old compatriots and I told them about how I am now clean – they laughed. We then came close to Albert park, woonga smoker's paradise, but my antennas weren't picking up the signal. It took until I stopped talking and looked at Mageba for me to realize that he was sweating profusely, and his face looked as if he was wearing a mask of himself, as if we were in some opera.

Zwide: Hhaybo mfowethu, what's going on?

Mageba: ey...*he showed me his arms which looked like a plucked chicken*

Zwide: *shocked*

Mageba: We are near where I used to smoke, it is right down the street.

Zwide: Lets go back to the centre. *we got on one of the night club quantums*

My suggestion is influenced by what I currently do in order to subdue the addiction and baNtu philosophy which teaches that, you remove a thorn by using another, "iva likhishwa ngelinye iva". Once an addict, always an addict and therefore even if you were to stay sober for twenty years, should you start experimenting again or have a moment of weakness where Mr Hungry overpowers you, you will have relapsed and gone back to square one – you will most probably sink deeper into addiction that before you originally quit. Why is this? Let's go back to our analogy: Mr Hungry is always famished, as I had already explained and by quitting, you have to subdue him such that you are under control. The problem is that he gets restless when you put him on an indefinite famine and by going through the triggers which used to go hand-in-hand with your substance seeking , just like Friday afternoon for an alcoholic or approaching a park that you used to smoke at for Mageba, the hungry fellow gains power over you and your internal environment, therefore it is such triggers which put you under moments of weakness. I realized this after I relapsed. The strategy which I employed when gaining control for the second time, is that after a few months clean, I then used marijuana to feed the hungry fellow every month or two, so that he doesn't fight me and try to strangle me whenever he gains some power over me. I used it after I hadn't touched it in a long time and so I knew that I would have a very low tolerance. The thing is, when you have a moment or days of weakness, it is like you are flipping a coin, should you pick heads and tails is facing up, you have lost and will have to watch as he devours everything in his path for the next few years until you gather enough strength to fight back again; it took me 7 years after relapsing to be able to gain some control again. How do I tame the beast? Well, I give him a bone to chew on. What you must first do when using marijuana, even if it is not for this cause, is decide why you are using it and then stick to that. So, for someone who is fighting to prevent a relapse from a more powerful substance, you must use it once or twice a month.

Some people attend AA meetings and it works for them, but everyone has their thing, and just like in spirituality, what works for one person might not necessarily work for another therefore it is the same with this method. The gist of this is microdosing. Another substance which I used successfully - after I got stronger and didn't need the strength of the medcinal plant - was non-alcoholic beer; as soon as I smell the beer after opening it and taste it in my mouth, Mr Hungry goes berserk with excitement, but he subsides very fast after he gulps down the dumpie in a matter of seconds. With marijuana I found that two pulls are enough a dosage if I medicate with it, but I don't forget that I am an addict, therefore I rarely keep it in the house after I have medicated. As the time goes I have been able to stay longer without the need to medicate but I know what I am dealing with and so I tend to buy 2 maybe for dumpies and just gulp them down at a bar just so I know that Mr Hungry will not sneak up on me. This dosage is what works best for me and so someone who has more weight than me might need three pulls. I used to abuse it and it in turn abused me back just like how another person might abuse food and end up stuck on their bed indefinitely. I do however feel that no matter how it treats you, you should never smoke weed every day and especially not plus minus 10 blunts a day, every day as I did, but that's just a personal opinion.

It is crucial to first educate yourself on the effects of different types of the plant. With recreational use marijuana in general, a sativa will give you energy, focus and is good for being social, which is why some athletes who want endurance - marathon runners and MMA fighters – will not hesitate to keep a few grams near during training. People who have depression and anxiety are known to choose this strain in order to alleviate themselves. An indica will generally make you relaxed and hungry; this is the classic effect of what people think of when they imagine someone who is "high". People who suffer from acute pain and seizures are known to benefit from use of this strain, as well as those who have nausea especially after chemotherapy amongst many other medical benefits. Buying from a merchant on the street means that you never know what you are getting nor the potency of the product.

TO NEW BEGINNINGS

The end of the second year and start of the third came to be and this was the time for me to go back to school. I hadn't applied anywhere but I wasn't worried either because I had been in such a situation before - when I was let go off the first time. Most schools were full and the ones that I had previously went to didn't want anything to do with me. I eventually found one that seemed to have space for me and everything was looking good up until they asked me where I used to school before and I mentioned the one which was around 70km away (I didn't have any report card from the one in Durban so I had to). The person whom I was speaking to mentioned that they know the principal from my school and had only good things to say him, all I could do was smile and nod my head with the occasional "yes…hahaha yes, yes". Long story short, I filled in all the documents and was even told which class I would be in but two days later I received a call from the school and then, abracadabra, there wasn't any space available anymore. It was late February now and it seemed as if I was destined to be a freelance kids rugby coach but then my mother told me to pack my clothes because we are leaving in the morning. I asked her where we were going and she said,

Mom: To school, what do you think?

We woke up at 4 o'clock in the morning and got ready for the hired bakkie to arrive. We departed around 06:00a.m for the trip to Nkandla and I estimated for the trip to take around 2 – 3 hours at most. Two hours passed, then three…next thing we were on this gravel road that meandered around the river and mountains. I was sitting in the car thinking that my mother had finally had enough of me and was looking for a location where she can just have me pushing up the daisies because we couldn't have still been going anywhere hospitable. I started planning my escape: obvious vele the old lady can't run so she wasn't going to catch me so it was probably going to be the driver who was going to make a move thus I moved left, such that I was behind the passenger seat. After more than four hours travelling, we finally saw the, beaten up, board that read of the name of the secondary school.

I had never seen such a place before; there was hardly any grass to be seen, the only way to describe it is to say it was a semi-desert, the air was dry and there seemed to be no wind whatsoever – upon looking around I realized that we are at a bottom of a valley and were surrounded by mountains, so there was probably katabatic and anabatic movement of air. The goats were all so fat and I was confused as to what they might be eating until I saw them at the school dumping area eating papers: I was baffled because I never thought that such existed, these goats were utterly devouring all the papers and so I assumed that their instinct told them that paper is from plant origin and thus they couldn't help themselves, but how they digest it was a mystery to me. We had to dodge a pair of Donkeys chasing one another, when we entered the school grounds. They seemed to be in a quarrel because they were running towards the exit and one was biting off the ones ear in a gruesome fashion. I wasn't shocked by the school buildings because they were not buildings at all: it was five rows of around 15 classes and most of them had shattered windows and no doors, then there was the school hall which resembled a homeless shelter for livestock. As soon as we got out of the car, it felt as if the sun just fell from the sky and decided to sit on our faces, asking us what we were doing there.

A call was made and ten minutes later, boom, a relative of mine (Sibalukhulu) that I last saw at a very tender age and he was a teacher at this school. Sibalukhulu took us to the headmaster's office where we waited for the big man. He walked in 15 minutes later and greeted us all, in the process shaking our hands one by one – what took me by surprise was that he actually shook with his left hand, and I thought, "yep, definitely what I expect from people in an area where goats eat paper". He asked me which grade had I wanted to go in and obviously I was there to complete my matric and disappear as soon as possible but upon hearing that I had been doing NCS as a curriculum, he immediately said that I have to go back to grade ten and it wasn't up for debate because now it had changed to CAPS therefore everything taught had changed,

Principal: It's either I take you in for grade ten or I don't take you at all.

I was dumbstruck, I could literally feel my blood doing summersaults and my left knee started shaking uncontrollably. My mind automatically started visualizing what I wanted out of my life and my body temperature went back to normal. I agreed. After signing the registration forms, Sibalukhulu took us to where he had already organized for me to stay thereafter my mother left and I had to go take my school stationary at school – What boggled my mind was finding that there were no school fees to be paid and the books were all also free. I was fortunate to see Dlaba, who had been a friend of mine early on when I was just new to the drinking lifestyle, he helped me carry my learning material and we caught up. I then went back to my newly adopted homestead, which had around four two-roomed flats and there was around five of us in the one that I was assigned to. For some reason, there was no electricity in the area and I was quite baffled by that, seeing as it was already 20 years after the 1994 promise of free electricity for all. What also got to me was the lack of running water which led to us having to go fetch water at the nearby borehole – others were not so lucky as to have a water source so close to them and they had to fetch water at the various streams which connected to the Tugela river.

Arriving to a new school almost a month after the opening date was quite awkward because I felt like I stuck out like a door handle but I quickly settled in and caught up with the little work that they had covered. Unwittingly, I stopped writing as well as meditating too, thus focused solely on school – I replaced these habits with doing and perfecting everything that we got for homework. Deep down, I stopped meditating because I thought that it would bring unnecessary attention to me. Intense studying was done for the first test because I had a point to prove to myself, although I was worried that my mind hadn't fully recovered. It was a physics test which I tied for second on and thus began my momentum like Juggernaut. Hindrances seemed to be from outside the classroom than from within. It was tough having to see schoolmates drinking and smoking every weekend while I just pretended to be unawares. High hopes ,on my side, were on there not being any hectic drugs but I couldn't have been further from the truth because pupils who were drug addicts from the cities and had been sent here as a form of rehabilitation by their parents, would bring a bunch of different kinds, there were ones which I had never had the opportunity to sample in my times – because I certainly would've done just– but luckily these would quickly run out a week or two after arrival from home.

To keep my mind off things I decided to start selling some Nice-Nice just like I had been doing early on when I wanted to maintain my lifestyle. My business quickly took off and I employed one off my roommates in no time, then later it was other people in the homestead. Some of the comrades stole from me though and so I had to fire them while accepting that my money will never return unless I wanted to fight. Before I knew it, I was swimming in money, but I didn't know what to do with it because all I ever spent on were internal environment altering substances throughout my teenage years and now I was 20 years old and sober. I started spending my time with Dlaba more and more and I would buy him alcohol whenever he was around. I started sensing bad blood among my peers towards me and I was caught up in petty fights with them. I really hated it because I had had my fair share of fights, especially whenever I had to visit the headquarters, so now it was just draining but I held fast nonetheless.

The many years which I had been under Mr Hungry's spell had

rendered me far underdeveloped when it came to my social skills and in exchange were traits which had been specialised for maximum acquisition of mind altering substances, this was heightened by how I had started from a young age to abuse them. Other fragment traits were from when I was a rugby player, which had me talking like I could beat everyone up but times had changed and I didn't have the physical presence which I once had. Acting "normal" was the hardest mission I ever had to complete because most of the behaviour had become instinctive, it was entrenched into my unconscious mind.

On the last week of the first term was 12 months since I came out of rehab and so I decided to celebrate my sobriety: the only way I knew how to, was through alcohol, so I called two of the people I was close to , including Dlaba and we bathed in showers of liquor with all my profits from the term. I thought that I had conquered the addiction and so drinking once or twice would not be a problem, but I couldn't have been more wrong. We went to school on the following day and after school, I bought more – we were drunk for the whole week: I had relapsed. I couldn't even contain myself when I got home because I would go to the local bar every chance that I got. The barman seemed to be more jovial now that I was back to drinking.

Upon returning to school, I had a massive downfall with some of the boys in my homestead and at this point I didn't even fight back. It was clear to me that there was never going to be any peace and so I quickly found a new place to stay overnight, in my bruised state. All of this really got to me but I bottled up the anger because in my head was a vision that overshadowed my reality. In the first week back, the school revealed the top 10 achievers in each grade and when they got to my grade, there I was on the stage, well and able to see in the eyes of my former housemates when they were staring at me. I visualized my dream, realized that my work was paying off and now that I was seeing the beginning of my manifestation I got more determined. My new homestead was neighbouring the school (although further away from the water source) and so I could wake up twenty minutes before the start of school. I spent time alone and reflected on what was going on and I realized that my sharpened memory was coming into play very well when it came to my studies. I learnt to tame my creativity when answering questions because it had now dawned on me that the memorandum wants you to bring back what they want and not your own take on it.

Overtime I spent lesser and lesser time studying and more time visualizing whatever was taught in class. It got to an extent that I would be making up my own questions and answering them without ever picking up a pen or paper. I spent most of my time alone even during lunch break at school and this is when I would be visualizing all that was taught: as we were being taught, I would close my eyes - sometimes teachers would shout at me and tell me to wake up – so I could easily turn it into a story in my head and then whenever I was alone outside of class, I would play that story in my head over and over until I would only be seeing the highlights. After the teachers were adamant that I should write down notes like everyone, I would wait until a paragraph is written and then summarize it into a line or two, right after transforming it into moving pictures in my head in a story format. Whenever I would be drinking during the weekends, I would be playing the same stories in my head while my companions would be telling each other stories of their own, relating to who did what with whom. I'll be honest, it got to a point where I was sick of it due to I was no longer in control but rather it was happening automatically because I had been doing this every single day till it became a habit – it was no different from addiction. It seemed that my weakness and high susceptibility to addiction was playing out to my advantage through this obsession.

The principal had been absent for the majority of the first term, so it was in the second that we really got to know him. As soon as his mouth opened during morning assembly, it was clear to every new learner why this school had been running so efficiently even without his presence in the first three months. His voice in speech form sounded like a fifteen thousand strong wildebeest stampede was fast approaching around the corner, to the school quad, and we were Mufasa. I listened in sheer awe as all my confusion relating to the environment that we were in was made into a mere speed bump compared to what we were to leave with at the end of our stay. I looked around and could no longer see anyone although I was in the middle of a thousand other learners, it was as if it were just me and him in a small room, and he had x-ray vision that allowed him to see all that I desired. Words cannot really dream of scratching the surface of the description of what I was seeing and feeling. I didn't know what was happening but all I knew was that I had to go to class and do the very best that I could so that I could make him proud. He then kept quiet and looked around for a second, then said,

Principal: You all look so beautiful my children, naze nabahle! When was the last time someone told you how beautiful you are? God has blessed me with such beautiful children this year. That being said, if you get out of line in my school, you will be disciplined so fast that you wish you never came here: I am here to mould a soldier that will leave here, grab life by the horns and show the whole world that he has been taught. Angiyena umuntu.

I needed a drink after what I had just experienced. I had been to three different high schools before this one, but this was the first time that I felt as if I belonged.

This place was survival of the fittest and so it was not long after that tensions flared, and another fight ensued, this time I had a rupture next to my eye. I had to visit the clinic in my drowsy and bloody state. Luckily my roommate was there to walk me because it was over five kilometres away, up and over a hilly dusty landscape. By the time we got there, at around 19h00, it was already closed but luckily there was someone there who took me in and called an ambulance just so I could get stitched up. The ambulance arrived over two hours later and I was off. When we got to the hospital a few hours later, I was told that I had to wait for the doctor who would arrive in the morning thus I was taken to an office that

I had to wait in until dawn. I finally got stitched up in the morning and was officially admitted in.

After I managed to charge my phone, I called my mother, told her everything and also requested that should I die in here, I don't want anyone to have my favourite boots which were in my wardrobe at home. The day after, I was let go, thus I had to leave. My mother instructed me to come back home so that I could recover but she had already decided that I was not going back to school. I couldn't fathom how I could just drop everything and waste another year. I had a vision, I had a dream, and nothing was going to stop me. I called some of my teachers and begged so that they would speak to her for me and I was successful. I went back there and picked up where I left off. The year ended with me swimming in a pool of distinctions.

I spent the holidays drinking and smoking cigarettes. I catered to staying as far away from any other substance. When school holidays ended, I went back to school but I wasn't the same person. I had broken a good habit and had overpowered it with old ones. My marks dropped by two distinctions in the first term back. I had to regain my composure. I was now staying at a different place and I was no longer in business because all my profit and working capital ended up at the tavern, I had to find other means to sustain myself now.

This year, one of the worst droughts in recent history was at full force, so the streams ran dry and my grandfather called me, in a sombre voice, to tell me how all his livestock was dying due to this El Nino. The closest water source was a bunch of puddles that were left in the streams that once flowed, most of the small pools were there because of groundwater seepage. The water had all kinds of living organisms in it, mostly some miniature worm-like creatures that were wiggling non-stop throughout; there was nothing that we could do about it, it is what we had to work with. There were six of us living in a two room house and there were a limited amount of buckets, worst of all, the cleaner source of water that was nearer was at the extremely salty borehole more than a kilometre away down the hill, therefore we couldn't handle the work needed to have a constant supply.

I decided to try out studying every day after school. I went to school strictly after having my supper, religiously, but that too was not enough so I combined it with my visualization then things started getting better and my made-up stories got better and memorable once more. I realized that I was now consuming more alcohol than I ever did before: sometimes everyday, but mostly we would drink the whole weekend with two of my roommates and by Monday, we would be hungover and utterly exhausted because drinking is all we did. My mind wouldn't be fully functional on the first two days of the week, Wednesday would be slightly better and I would be ready to take on tasks by Thursday, Friday would be a breeze but as soon as the final bell rang, Mr Hungry would take over my mind and we would be scheming on how we would get money to sustain our bottomless pit. I didn't know what to do about this, nor how to overcome it but I did know that I needed to drink some more: so I did.

We, as a school, were lucky to get help from a state owned enterprise in the form of a few storage tanks and probably the only working tap in the area : It availed water that was automatically sucked from the water-table below, using the school generator. More of us were now able to get clean water and the line would be shorter than the one at the original borehole area. This allowed one to go to school with a bucket and books so as to be able to come back with water to the homestead in the evenings, after studying. A distinguishing character of the school was the intense weekend classes – throughout my schooling days I thought that weekends were just for fun, but this was not the case here. These used to be counter revolutionary when it came to our addiction because we had to come to school with a little alcohol in our system on Saturdays. If we were lucky, classes would finish before noon and we would be able to head straight to the tavern afterwards, most of the time, whoever was in class would head straight to the tavern after class and obviously the camaraderies would be already there.

Things got extreme in matric. The pressure tends to get unbearable but visualizing the dream gave me mental steroids. We would be expected on school premises at 06:00am every weekday, be allowed to leave at 15:00pm and then come back at 18:00pm until 20:00pm and that's just the science classes – the commerce classes had it far worse. In order to handle the work, one had to drink in a revolutionary method: As soon as the alcohol was purchased, I would drink like there is no tomorrow, sipping after short intervals so that my body isn't able to breakdown the ethanol fast enough and this causes the body to shutdown in a spectacular blackout not long after. I would then have had drunk far less and would have rested far more than everyone.

This allowed me to be able to wake up earlier and be able to watch all the short stories that I had created in my head, repeatedly, and if there was something which I wasn't sure about, I would then open a book to check the notes for a few seconds – my roommates thought that I only studied for two minutes but it was more like twenty if you add the visualizations. The mind has a way of finding solutions and methods that will allow you to reach your goals if you saturate your thoughts with what you intend to achieve. What seems impossible to others will just happen automatically to you. I never decided to do things the way which I was doing them but it was the human mind which just combined all the skills which I had developed during my time as a dropout and sharpened them in order for them to make the cut – all this was possible because most of my days were spent thinking about my goal, even when I was engaging in substance use.

This was solidified when the final exams were near and due to the anxiety build-up, now that it was game time, my substance use heightened to an all new level; I even stopped visualizing because even the thought of it made me sick and the medicine was alcohol. I even sold most of my belongings during exam time, in order to stay drunk as possible, all it did was to give Mr Hungry more power. I persisted with this behaviour until the end of the final examinations – I was only sober on the mornings of the exams and then would go back to drowning myself right after writing.

In the same way that you pay money to buy bread at the store, the price for achieving a goal comes from self-discipline which you have to exercise every single day, you have no choice but to pay the price. Once you think that you have arrived and stop paying the price, it is then that you fall down the mountain like I later did right after my matric. You have to be in control of your internal environment and give it the same amount of attention which a women gives herself in the morning as she prepares to go out, you need to moisturize your soul and brush away the plague of negativity. When I was summoned to get an award for being in the top 100 matric achievers in the region and my name was called up to the stage, right in front of me was the DP, sitting there almost looking right through me.

Made in the USA
Columbia, SC
20 May 2022